KT-527-140

why ? why ? why ?

Who cuddled the first teddy bear?

Rosie Greenwood

p

This is a Parragon Book
First published in 2001

Parragon
Queen Street House
4 Queen Street
Bath BA1 1HE, UK

Produced by

David West Children's Books
7 Princeton Court
55 Felsham Road
Putney
London SW15 1AZ

British Library Cataloguing-in-Publication Data

A catalogue record for this book is available from the British Library.

ISBN 0-75255-364-X

Printed in Italy

Designers
Aarti Parmar, Rob Shone, Fiona Thorne

Illustrator
Neil Reed (Allied Artists)

Cartoonist
Peter Wilks (SGA)

Editor
James Pickering

CONTENTS

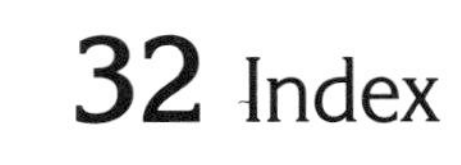

Who played with the first dolls?

The first doll-like figures weren't made for playing with – they were used thousands of years ago in religious ceremonies, by grown-ups.

The first children to play with dolls lived more than 2,000 years ago, in Ancient Greece.

Who cuddled the first teddy bears?

Our great-grandparents were the first children to have soft, furry teddy bears. They were first made in Germany and the United States in the early 1900s.

When were the first train sets made?

Toy train sets were first made a few years after the world's first real railway line opened in 1825.

TRUE OR FALSE?

Barbie is older than Action Man.

TRUE. The first Barbie doll was sold in 1959, Action Man in 1964.

Teddy bears are named after a boy called Edward.

FALSE. They were named after the US president Theodore Roosevelt in 1902. His nickname was Teddy.

Who baked the first birthday cakes?

Birthday cakes were first made by the Ancient Greeks more than 2,000 years ago, to honour their Moon goddess, Artemis. Candles were put on top to copy the light of the Moon and the stars.

Where did fireworks first go bang?

Fireworks were invented in China more than 1,000 years ago. Bamboo tubes were packed with an explosive called gunpowder, which went off with a bang when it caught fire.

When were the first Christmas cards sent?

People began buying Christmas cards to send to friends and family in the 1840s. The pictures on the first cards were drawn by an English artist called John Calcott Horsely.

TRUE OR FALSE?

Sticky postage stamps appeared in the 1840s.

TRUE. The first was the British Penny Black of 1840.

Christmas trees were first decorated in Germany.

TRUE. The idea began to spread around the world in the 1830s.

Where were hamburgers first sold?

Although they're named after the German town of Hamburg, the first hamburgers in buns were sold in the United States in 1904. The first McDonald's opened in California 44 years later.

What does Coca-Cola have to do with headaches?

When Coca-Cola was invented in the 1880s, it was sold as a cure for headaches. It wasn't a soft drink and it wasn't fizzy!

Who invented ice cream?

No one knows who came up with the idea of turning ice into yummy food. We do know that the Chinese and the Romans were licking at frozen fruit juice more than 2,000 years ago, and that milk was first made into ice cream about 500 years ago.

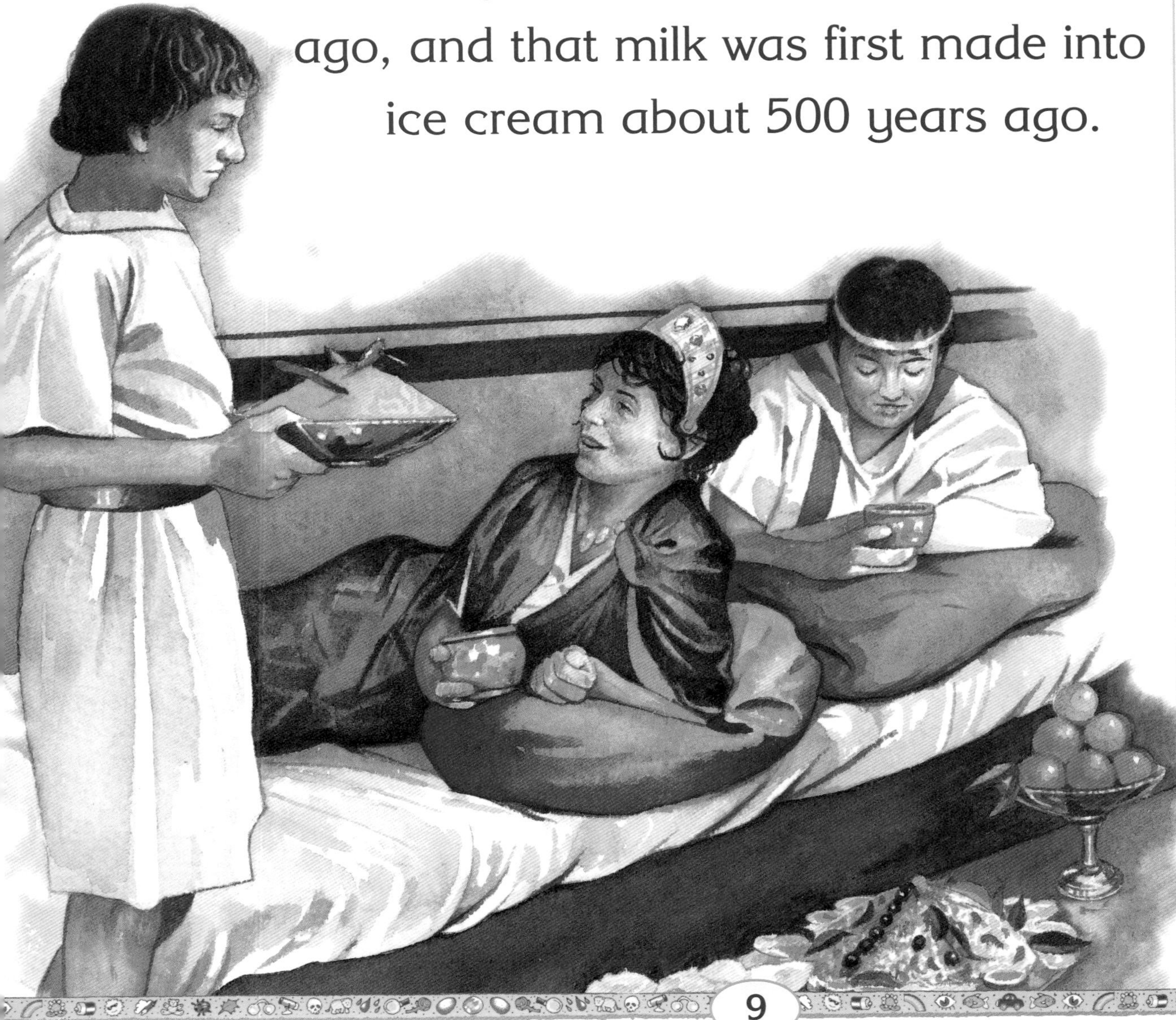

TRUE OR FALSE?

The Romans invented ice-cream cones.

FALSE. Cones were first sold in the United States in 1904.

Pizzas were invented in the United States.

FALSE. The people of Naples, Italy, first tucked into them over 200 years ago.

Who invented the dishwasher?

An American called Mrs Cockran first thought of making a machine to take the hard work out of washing up, back in 1879. Modern dishwashers are powered by electricity, but Mrs Cockran's had a steam engine.

Who put the pop into toasters?

Electric toasters were invented in 1913, but people were always burning their breakfast because the first machines didn't pop the toast out. The pop-up toaster was the brainwave of an American called Charles Strife, and it was first sold in 1926.

Who put popcorn into the first microwave?

An American scientist called Percy Spencer invented the microwave oven in the early 1940s. He tested his ideas out by using microwaves to cook popcorn.

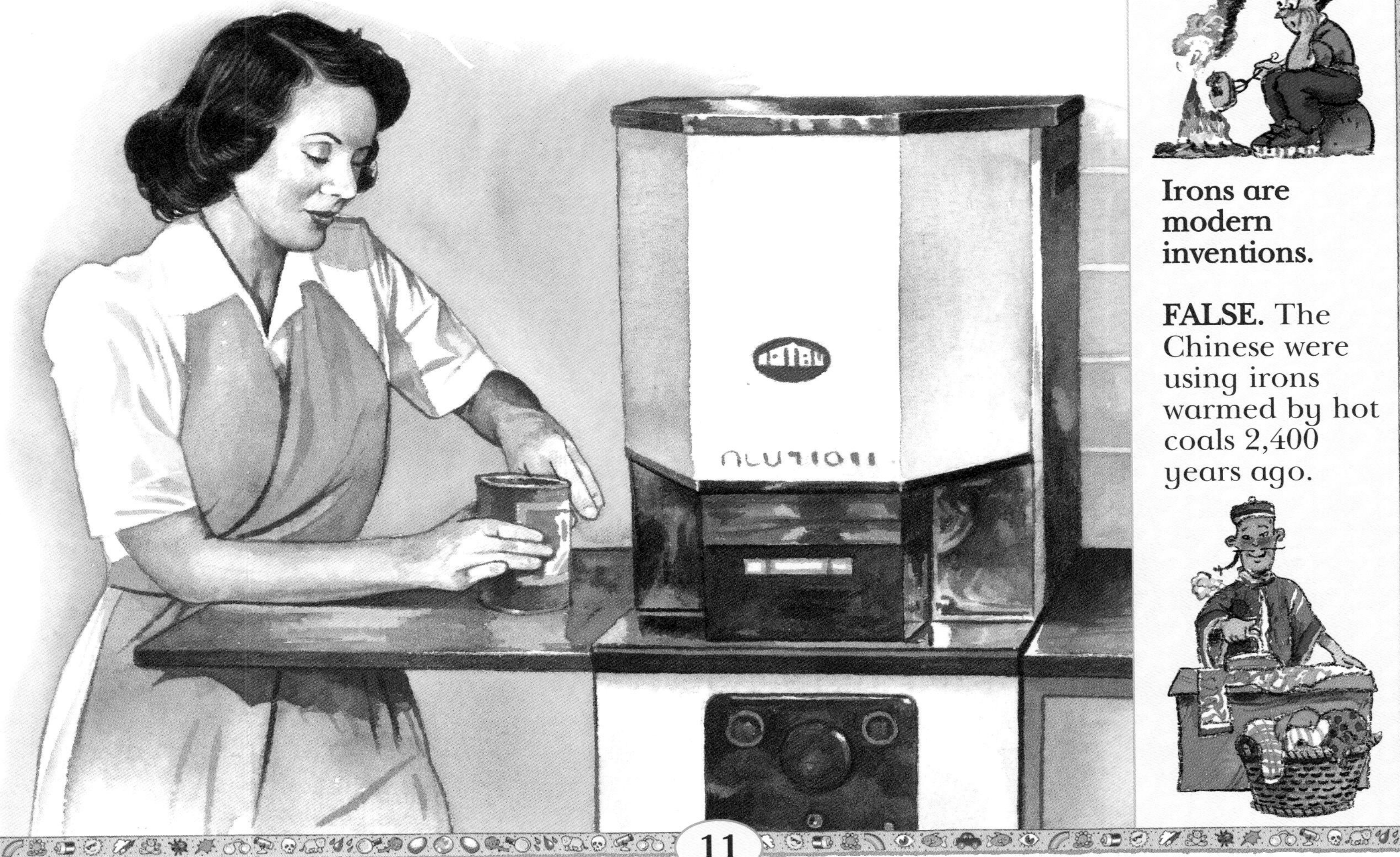

TRUE OR FALSE?

People didn't eat toast before electric toasters were invented.

FALSE. They made toast by holding bread on a toasting fork in front of the fire.

Irons are modern inventions.

FALSE. The Chinese were using irons warmed by hot coals 2,400 years ago.

Who wore the first jeans?

Jeans were made as tough work trousers for gold miners in the United States. They were invented in the 1850s by a man called Levi Strauss. Levi jeans, in many styles and colours, are still worn all over the world today.

When were zips invented?

People had to fiddle with buttons or hooks-and-eyes before zips took off. The zip was invented in the 1890s, but the first one wasn't an instant hit because it still used rows of hooks-and-eyes. Zips with teeth came along a few years later.

Who first looked cool in sunglasses?

Chinese lawcourt judges were wearing shades more than 900 years ago, to hide their eyes so people couldn't tell what they were thinking. The lenses were made from tea-coloured slivers of a stone called quartz.

TRUE OR FALSE?

The first jeans were blue.

FALSE. Although Levi Strauss soon switched to hard-wearing blue denim, the first jeans were made of brown cloth.

The idea for Velcro came from a wild thistle seed.

TRUE. It was invented in the 1940s, inspired by the hooked seeds of the burdock thistle.

How many wheels did the first cycle have?

When cycles were first made in the 1640s, they had four wheels. One of the earliest two-wheelers appeared in 1818, but it was hard work – you had to push it along with your feet because it didn't have pedals. The first pedal-powered bicycle was built in about 1839, by a Scot called Kirkpatrick Macmillan.

When were roller skates invented?

Roller skates were invented in the 1700s, but no one knows who by. We do know that by about 1760, a Belgian called Joseph Merlin was making them in London.

TRUE OR FALSE?

Joseph Merlin was the inventor of in-line skates.

FALSE. In-line skates were developed in the 1980s by Americans Brennan and Scott Olson.

What do skateboards have to do with surfing?

Skateboards were first sold in the early 1960s. They were the brainwave of American surfers who wanted a way of surfing on land as well as on ocean waves.

Prams came before bicycles.

TRUE. Prams were invented in China as long as 1,200 years ago.

When was paper invented?

The earliest kind of paper was made by the Ancient Egyptians at about the same time as they built the first pyramids – a whopping 5,000 years ago. Egyptian paper was made from a plant called papyrus. The kind of paper we use today was invented in China nearly 1,900 years ago.

Who printed the first books?

The Chinese came up with all sorts of brilliant inventions, including printing the first books more than 1,100 years ago. It was another 550 years before the idea took off in Europe. Before printing was invented, people wrote and illustrated books by hand.

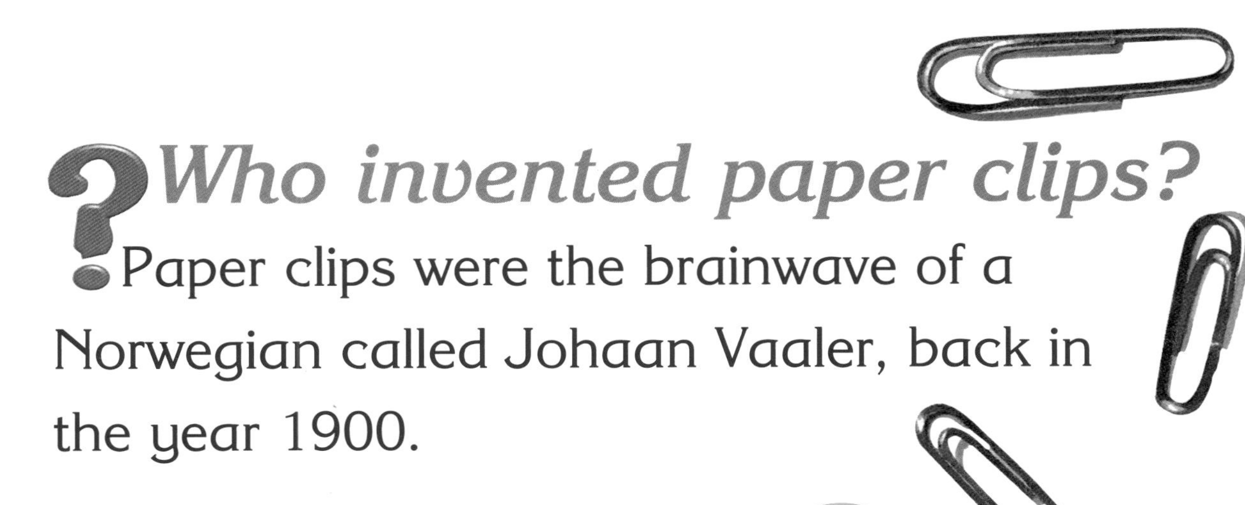

Who invented paper clips?

Paper clips were the brainwave of a Norwegian called Johaan Vaaler, back in the year 1900.

TRUE OR FALSE?

Scissors were invented by the Chinese.

TRUE. The Chinese invented scissors over 2,200 years ago.

The Chinese invented ink.

FALSE. The Ancient Egyptians did, just before they invented papyrus paper.

Where is the world's oldest pinball machine?

Pinball was probably invented in Spain, because the oldest machine is in the Spanish city of Barcelona. It's made of wood, and it was built as long ago as 1449.

Did the Americans invent baseball?

No, an early form of baseball was being played in England by the 1700s. The Americans did develop the modern game, though, and they came up with the first set of rules in 1845.

Where was the first game of football played?

An early game of football was played in China, more than 2,000 years ago. Hardly anyone stuck to the rules, though. In Europe, no one bothered with rules until the early 1800s, when rugby football was invented at England's Rugby School.

TRUE OR FALSE?

Soccer was invented in England.

TRUE. Soccer rules were first drawn up in England, way back in 1848.

Tennis was invented in England.

FALSE. Tennis was first played with rackets in France, in the early 1400s.

? *Who first flushed a toilet?*

The story of the modern flushing toilet begins in 1589, when an Englishman called Sir John Harrington designed one for his home. Flushing toilets were a great luxury to begin with. The toilet Harrington made for his godmother, Queen Elizabeth I, was even said to have had goldfish in the water tank!

? Who built bath-houses?

The Romans built magnificent public bath-houses, where they would go to exercise, meet friends and wash in hot and cold water. Some bath-houses were enormous – the Caracalla Baths in Rome had room for 1,600 bathers!

TRUE OR FALSE?

People once cleaned their teeth with pig bristles.

TRUE. The Chinese used pig bristles in the first toothbrushes, about 500 years ago.

Tubes of toothpaste were first sold 500 years ago.

FALSE. Toothpaste tubes first appeared in the 1890s.

Why were plasters invented?

An American called Earle E. Dickson made the first plasters for his wife, in 1920. She was always cutting herself when she was doing the cooking, and he was fed up with having to bandage her fingers.

Who were the first dentists?

The first professional dentists lived in Ancient Egypt more than 5,000 years ago. It was another 3,000 years before a basic dental drill was invented, though – before that, dentists simply yanked any bad teeth out!

? When were thermometers first used?

An Italian called Sanctorius was the first person to use a thermometer to take someone's temperature, more than 400 years ago.

TRUE OR FALSE?

Egyptian dentists made false teeth.

TRUE. A dentist called Neferites was making false teeth from ivory 4,600 years ago.

The Egyptians invented ambulances.

FALSE. Frenchman Dominique-Jean Larrey organised the first ambulance service in 1792.

Who made the first music?

No one knows who sang the first song or blew the first pipes, but the first tunes were written down as long as 2,200 years ago. They were carved into clay slabs by the Mesopotamians – people who lived in the land we now call Iraq.

Who played the first piano?

Although piano-like instruments were made in ancient times, the first true piano wasn't built until 1698. The first person to try it out was its maker, an Italian called Bartolomeo Cristofori.

? When were electric guitars invented?

Stringed instruments have been played for thousands of years, but the first electric guitar, a Rickenbacker, wasn't sold until the early 1930s.

Electric guitars can be played loudly and can easily be heard above other noisy instruments in the band.

TRUE OR FALSE?

The first lullaby was sung 4,300 years ago.

TRUE. We know the words, but not the tune. It was written in Mesopotamia.

CDs were invented in the 1930s.

FALSE. They first went on sale in the early 1980s.

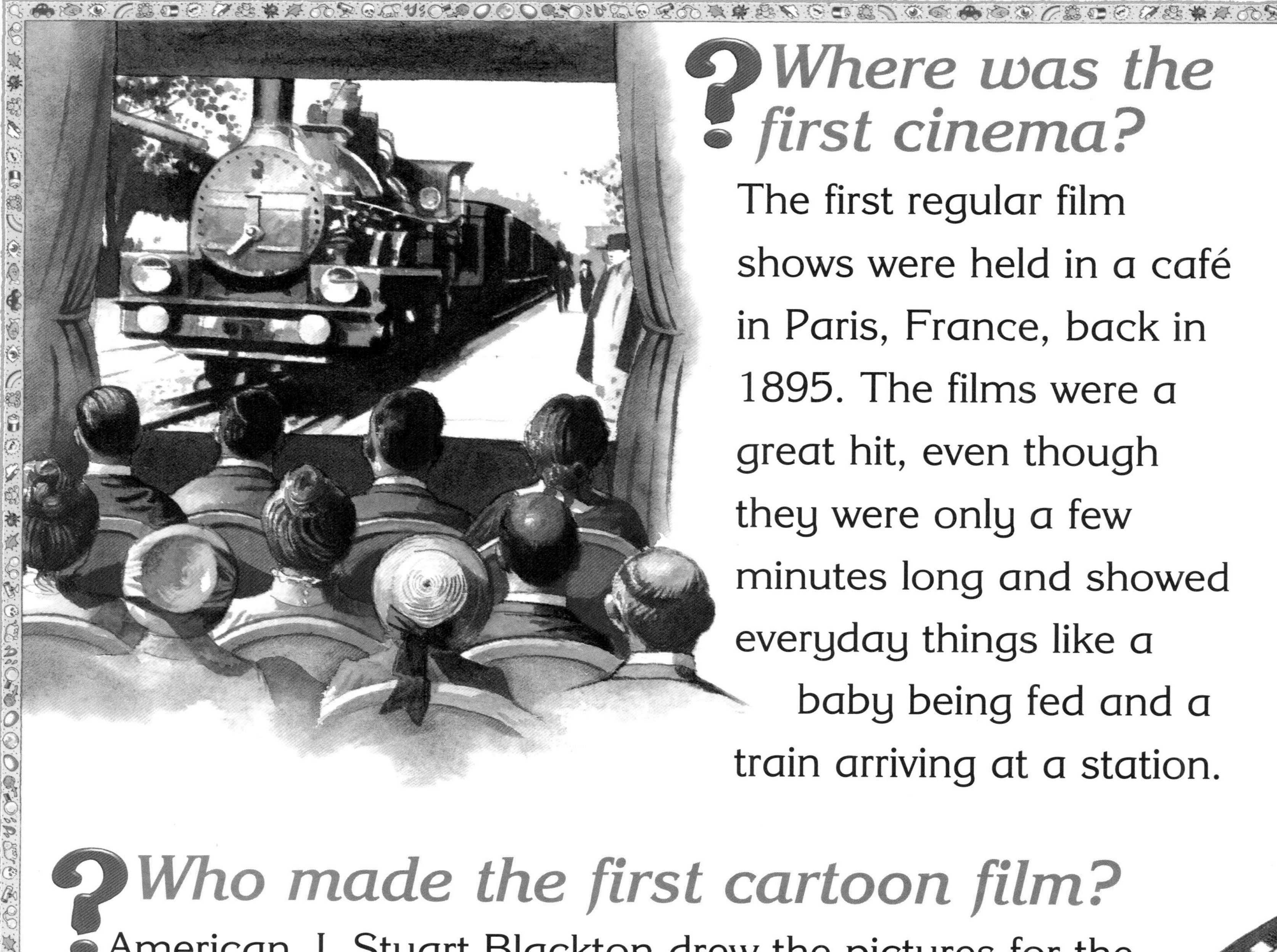

Where was the first cinema?

The first regular film shows were held in a café in Paris, France, back in 1895. The films were a great hit, even though they were only a few minutes long and showed everyday things like a baby being fed and a train arriving at a station.

Who made the first cartoon film?

American J. Stuart Blackton drew the pictures for the first cartoon, in the early 1900s. The most famous cartoon character, Mickey Mouse, first appeared in a film called Steamboat Willie in 1928.

What was the first video game?

The first video game was called Pong, and it was invented in 1972 by Norman Bushell. You could play Pong against another person, or against the machine itself.

TRUE OR FALSE?

You could hear the first movies.

FALSE. The Jazz Singer, from 1927, was the first successful talking picture.

Television came before cinema.

FALSE. The first television programmes were shown in the 1930s.

?What were the first words spoken into a telephone?

In March 1876, Scotsman Alexander Graham Bell was testing out his invention for a telephone when he spilt some chemicals on his clothes. He called for his assistant: 'Mr Watson, come here. I want you!' Even though Watson was in another room, he heard every word down the phone and rushed to help.

? Who switched on the first electric light bulb?

The problem with early electric light bulbs was that they burnt out very quickly. The first people to come up with successful electric light bulbs were Englishman Joseph Swan in 1878, and American Thomas Edison a year later.

TRUE OR FALSE?

Bell invented the answering machine.

FALSE. Valdemar Poulsen from Denmark came up with the idea in 1898.

Edison was the first person to record and play sounds.

TRUE. He invented a machine called a phonograph in the 1870s.

Who built the first computer?

The world's first electronic computer was designed and built in 1946 in the United States, by a team led by John Mauchly and J. Presper Eckert. The computer was called ENIAC and it was a monster. It filled an entire room and weighed more than six elephants.

When was the Internet born?

The American armed forces began work on the idea of an Internet in the late 1960s. Universities and businesses set up their own networks during the 1970s and '80s, but ordinary people only began using the Internet in the early 1990s.

When was virtual reality invented?

Wearing a virtual reality helmet puts you right inside a computer game – you're bang in the middle of the action. Virtual reality games appeared in the late 1990s. Virtual reality is also used to train athletes, doctors, pilots and even firefighters.

TRUE OR FALSE?

Washing machines have computers inside them.

TRUE. They are run by tiny computers called microchips.

The first personal computer was an Apple.

FALSE. The Altair was the first, in 1975.

Index